SCHOLASTIC

Solve-the-Riddle
Phonics Practice

Deborah Schecter

New York • Toronto • London • Auckland • Sydney
Mexico City • New Delhi • Hong Kong • Buenos Aires

Teaching Resources

Cover design by Maria Lilja
Interior design by Solas
Illustrations by Maxie Chambliss, Rusty Fletcher, James Graham Hale, and Anne Kennedy
ISBN-13: 978-0-545-23968-4
ISBN-10: 0-545-23968-0

2 3 4 5 6 7 8 9 10   40   17 16 15 14 13 12 11

Contents

What the Research Says

In his book *Phonics From A to Z: A Practical Guide*, 2nd ed. (Scholastic, 2006), reading specialist Wiley Blevins notes that the faster children can decode words, and the more words they recognize by sight, the more fluent they become, leaving more time and energy to focus on comprehension (Freedman and Calfee, 1984; LaBerge and Samuels, 1974). Blevins cites Cunningham's (1995) observation that the brain works as a "pattern detector." Since blends, digraphs, and many vowel sounds contain reliable sound-spelling patterns, learning to recognize their common patterns increases and improves word recognition skills.

About This Book

Welcome to *Solve-the-Riddle Phonics Practice*! The engaging riddle activities in this collection offer a unique and motivating way to help students practice the basic sound-letter relationships needed in decoding, comprehension, writing, and spelling. Chosen especially for their appeal to primary-grade students, each riddle activity targets a specific phonics skill, such as short and long vowels, variant vowel patterns, *r*-controlled vowels and diphthongs, and initial- and ending-consonant clusters and digraphs. As students enjoy solving these rib-tickling riddles, they'll build important phonics skills that will help them become confident, independent readers.

Introducing the Activities

1. Read aloud a riddle. For example, Riddle 1 (page 6) asks, "What flying animal is found at baseball games?" Then point out the phonics focus at the top of the page (*short a*). Explain that the answer to this riddle is a word that features the short-*a* sound.

2. Review the directions. To solve the riddle, students work with words that contain the same vowel sound. They identify each picture below the riddle, and then write the short-*a* word it represents in the spaces and boxes provided.

3. In the Solve the Riddle! section, students write the letters from the boxes, in order, to spell out the solution to the riddle. *What flying animal is found at baseball games? A bat!*

4. To ensure students understand how to complete the activities, have them try solving Riddle 2 on their own.

5. Extend learning by helping students explore the play on words, puns, and multiple meanings in many of the riddles.

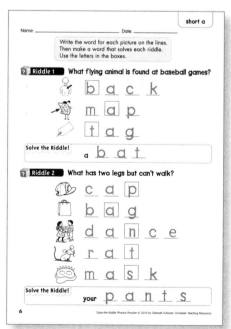

Meeting the Standards—Supporting RTI

The activities in this book help meet key state and national language arts standards (see below), and can be used to support the Response to Intervention (RTI) efforts in your school. RTI, a federal initiative, is a three-tier intervention approach in which educators provide early screening and specific, targeted intervention, particularly in reading, for at-risk students. Conceived as a prevention model, the goal of RTI is to achieve success for all students. The riddle activities offer students targeted practice in specific phonics skills to support their instructional needs and provide the repeated practice they need to attain mastery.

Teaching Tips

- Use your students' different ability levels as a guide when assigning the activity sheets.

- The activities are flexible and easy to use for independent work, at centers, or as day starters or homework.

Meeting the Language Arts Standards

Connections to the McREL Language Arts Standards

The activities in this book are designed to support the following language arts standards outlined by Mid-continent Research for Education and Learning (McREL), a nationally recognized, nonprofit organization that collects and synthesizes national and state K–12 curriculum standards.

Reading
Employs the general skills and strategies of the reading process

- Uses mental images based on pictures and print to aid in comprehension of text

- Uses basic elements of phonetic analysis (for example, common letter/sound relationships, beginning consonants, vowel sounds, blends, word patterns) to decode unknown words

- Uses basic elements of structural analysis, such as spelling patterns, to decode unknown words

Writing
Employs grammatical and mechanical conventions in writing

- Uses conventions of spelling in writing (for example, spells phonetically regular words; uses letter-sound relationships; spells basic short vowel, long vowel, r-controlled, and consonant blend patterns)

Source: Kendall, J. S. & Marzano, R. J. (2004). *Content knowledge: A compendium of standards and benchmarks for K–12 education.* Aurora, CO: Mid-continent Research for Education and Learning Online database: http://www.mcrel.org/standards-benchmarks/

Connections to the Reading First Program

The activities in this book are also designed to support you in implementing the recommendations of the Reading First Program, authorized by the U.S. Department of Education's No Child Left Behind Act. The National Reading Panel has identified the five key areas of reading instruction as follows:

- **Phonemic Awareness** The ability to hear, identify, and manipulate phonemes—the sounds of spoken language

- **Phonics Development** Understanding the predictable relationship between phonemes and graphemes—the letters and spellings that represent those sounds in written language—helps readers recognize familiar words accurately and automatically and to decode unfamiliar words

- **Vocabulary Development** The ability to store information about the meanings and pronunciation of words necessary for communicating, including vocabulary for listening, speaking, reading, and writing

- **Fluency** The ability to read text accurately and quickly that allows readers to recognize words and comprehend at the same time

- **Comprehension** The ability to understand and gain meaning from material read

Source: *Guidance for the Reading First Program.* (U.S. Department of Education Office of Elementary and Secondary Education, 2002)

Name: _____   Date: _____

> Write the word for each picture on the lines.
> Then make a word that solves each riddle.
> Use the letters in the boxes.

?? Riddle 1   What flying animal is found at baseball games?

[□] ___ ___ ___

___ [□] ___

[□] ___

Solve the Riddle!

a ___ ___ ___

?? Riddle 2   What has two legs but can't walk?

___ ___ [□]

___ [□] ___

___ ___ [□] ___

___ ___ [□] ___

___ ___ [□] ___

Solve the Riddle!

your ___ ___ ___ ___

Solve-the-Riddle Phonics Practice © 2010 by Deborah Schecter. Scholastic Teaching Resources

Name: _____ Date: _____

> Write the word for each picture on the lines.
> Then make a word that solves each riddle.
> Use the letters in the boxes.

?? Riddle 3   What will you always find when you reach in your pocket?

[ham]   ☐ ___

[cat]   ___ ☐ ___

[fan]   ___ ___ ☐

[dad]   ☐ ___ ___

Solve the Riddle!

your   ___ ___ ___ ___

?? Riddle 4   What do you lose when you stand up?

[clam]   ___ ☐ ___ ___

[mat]   ___ ☐ ___

[pan]   ☐ ___ ___

Solve the Riddle!

your   ___ ___ ___

Name: _____ Date: _____

Write the word for each picture on the lines.
Then make a word that solves each riddle.
Use the letters in the boxes.

? ? Riddle 5   **What do frogs make notes on?**

___ ___ ___ ☐

___ ☐ ___ ☐

___ ___ ___ ☐ ___

☐ ___ ___

Solve the Riddle!

lily ___ ___ ___ ___

? ? Riddle 6   **What keeps TV stars cool?**

☐ ___ ___ ___

___ ___ ☐ ___

___ ___ ☐

___ ___ ☐ ___

Solve the Riddle!

their ___ ___ ___

Name: _____   Date: _____

Write the word for each picture on the lines.
Then make a word that solves each riddle.
Use the letters in the boxes.

? ? Riddle 7   What room does a bear like best?

___ ___ ___ [ ]

___ [ ] ___ ___

___ ___ [ ] ___

Solve the Riddle!

the   ___ ___ ___

? ? Riddle 8   What has four legs, but only one foot?

___ ___ [ ]

___ [ ] ___ ___

[ ] ___ ___ ___

Solve the Riddle!

a   ___ ___ ___

Name: _____ Date: _____

> Write the word for each picture on the lines.
> Then make a word that solves each riddle.
> Use the letters in the boxes.

Riddle 9   What do you call pigs who write to each other?

____ ____ ____ ☐

____ ☐ ____

☐ ____ ____

Solve the Riddle!

____ ____ ____ pals

Riddle 10   What runs around a yard but does not move?

____ ____ ☐

____ ☐ ____

☐ ____ ____ ____

☐ ____ ____

____ ☐ ____

Solve the Riddle!

a ____ ____ ____ ____ ____

10

Solve-the-Riddle Phonics Practice © 2010 by Deborah Schecter. Scholastic Teaching Resources

Name: _____ Date: _____

Write the word for each picture on the lines.
Then make a word that solves each riddle.
Use the letters in the boxes.

Riddle 11 What do you get when you jump
in the Red Sea?

□ ___ ___ ___

___ □ ___

___ □ ___ ___

Solve the Riddle!

___ ___ ___ !

Riddle 12 What has to be broken before it can be used?

10 ___ □ ___

___ ___ □

□ ___ ___

Solve the Riddle!

an ___ ___ ___

Name: _____ Date: _____

Write the word for each picture on the lines.
Then make a word that solves each riddle.
Use the letters in the boxes.

? ? Riddle 13 What's inside a pen but is not ink?

☐ _ _

_ ☐ _

_ _ ☐

Solve the Riddle!

a _ _ _

? ? Riddle 14 What do you call a baby chick with a cold?

☐ _ _ _

_ ☐ _ _

☐ _ _

_ _ ☐

Solve the Riddle!

a _ _ _ _ **chick**

Solve-the-Riddle Phonics Practice © 2010 by Deborah Schecter. Scholastic Teaching Resources

Name: _____ Date: _____

Write the word for each picture on the lines.
Then make a word that solves each riddle.
Use the letters in the boxes.

Riddle 15 What did the apple tree say to the farmer?

___ ___ □

___ □ ___

□ ___ ___ ___

___ ___ ___ □ ___

Solve the Riddle!

Don't ___ ___ ___ ___ on me!

Riddle 16 What do snakes do after a fight?

___ ___ □

___ □ ___ ___

□ ___ ___ ___

___ ___ □ ___

Solve the Riddle!

___ ___ ___ ___ and make up.

Name: _____ Date: _____

Write the word for each picture on the lines.
Then make a word that solves each riddle.
Use the letters in the boxes.

? ? Riddle 17 What happens when you chop down a tuna tree?

☐ ___ ___

___ ☐ ___

☐ ___ ___

☐ ___ ___

Solve the Riddle!

You get ___ ___ ___ ___ sticks.

? ? Riddle 18 What is red and white?

☐ ___ ___ ___

___ ☐ ___

___ ___ ___ ☐

___ ___ ☐

Solve the Riddle!

___ ___ ___ ___

Solve-the-Riddle Phonics Practice © 2010 by Deborah Schecter. Scholastic Teaching Resources

Name: _____ Date: _____

Write the word for each picture on the lines.
Then make a word that solves each riddle.
Use the letters in the boxes.

? ? Riddle 19   What do you call a dog with a fever?

☐ __ __

__ ☐ __ __

☐ __ __

Solve the Riddle!

a __ __ __ dog

? ? Riddle 20   What does a baby ear of corn call its dad?

__ __ ☐

__ ☐ __

☐ __ __

Solve the Riddle!

__ __ __ corn

Name: _____ Date: _____

Write the word for each picture on the lines.
Then make a word that solves each riddle.
Use the letters in the boxes.

? ? Riddle 21 What is the most silly name for a zebra?

_____ ___ ___ ___

_____ ___ ___ ___

___ _____ ___

_____ ___ ___

Solve the Riddle!

___ ___ ___ ___

? ? Riddle 22 What kind of mail do fish get?

_____ ___

___ _____ ___

_____ ___

_____ ___

Solve the Riddle!

post – ___ ___ ___ ___

Solve-the-Riddle Phonics Practice © 2010 by Deborah Schecter. Scholastic Teaching Resources

Name: _____ Date: _____

> Write the word for each picture on the lines.
> Then make a word that solves each riddle.
> Use the letters in the boxes.

Riddle 23 What wears a coat all winter and pants in summer?

[ ] ___ ___ ___

___ ___ [ ] ___

___ ___ [ ]

Solve the Riddle!
a ___ ___ ___

Riddle 24 What word has the most letters?

___ ___ ___ [ ]

___ [ ] ___

___ ___ [ ]

Solve the Riddle!
mail ___ ___ ___

Name: _____ Date: _____

Write the word for each picture on the lines.
Then make a word that solves each riddle.
Use the letters in the boxes.

Riddle 25   Who visits an elephant when it loses a tooth?

____ ____ [ ]

____ [ ] ____

[ ] ____ ____

____ ____ [ ] ____

Solve the Riddle!

the ____ ____ ____ ____ fairy

Riddle 26   What is the smallest room?

____ [ ] ____ ____

1
+1
___
2
____ [ ] ____

____ ____ [ ]

[ ] ____ ____

Solve the Riddle!

a ____ ____ ____ room

18

Name: _____ Date: _____

Write the word for each picture on the lines.
Then make a word that solves each riddle.
Use the letters in the boxes.

Riddle 27 What did the dog say to the flea?

[ ] ___ ___

___ [ ] ___

___ ___ [ ]

Solve the Riddle!

You ___ ___ ___ me!

Riddle 28 What goes under your feet and over your head?

[ ] ___ ___

___ [ ] ___

___ ___ [ ]

___ ___ ___ [ ]

Solve the Riddle!

a ___ ___ ___ ___ rope

Heading

Name: _____ Date: _____

Write the word for each picture on the lines.
Then make a word that solves each riddle.
Use the letters in the boxes.

Riddle 29 What did one plate say to the other plate?

Solve the Riddle! __ __ __ __ __ is on me!

Riddle 30 Where do bear cubs like to take a bath?

Solve the Riddle! in a cub __ __ __

20

Solve-the-Riddle Phonics Practice © 2010 by Deborah Schecter. Scholastic Teaching Resources

Name: _____ Date: _____

> Write the word for each picture on the lines.
> Then make a word that solves each riddle.
> Use the letters in the boxes.

? ? Riddle 31 **What goes up and never comes down?**

___ [ ] ___ ___

[ ] ___ ___ ___

___ ___ [ ] ___

Solve the Riddle!

your ___ ___ ___

? ? Riddle 32 **How can you fix a broken tomato?**

___ ___ [ ] ___

___ [ ] ___

[ ] ___ ___

[ ] ___ ___

___ ___ ___ [ ]

Solve the Riddle!

Use tomato ___ ___ ___ ___ ___ .

Name: _____ Date: _____

Write the word for each picture on the lines.
Then make a word that solves each riddle.
Use the letters in the boxes.

Riddle 33   What always follows a horse?

_____ _____ ☐ _____

_____ ☐ _____

_____ _____ _____ ☐ _____

☐ _____

Solve the Riddle!

its ____ ____ ____ ____

Riddle 34   How does a flag say hello?

☐ _____ _____ _____

_____ ☐ _____

☐ _____ _____

_____ _____ ☐

Solve the Riddle!

It ____ ____ ____ ____ s.

Solve-the-Riddle Phonics Practice © 2010 by Deborah Schecter. Scholastic Teaching Resources

Name: _____ Date: _____

Write the word for each picture on the lines.
Then make a word that solves each riddle.
Use the letters in the boxes.

? Riddle 35 What kind of coat has no buttons or pockets?

_ _ _ □

_ _ □ □ _

_ _ □ _

□ _ _ _ _

Solve the Riddle!

a coat of ___ ___ ___ ___ ___

? Riddle 36 How is your hand like a hardware store?

_ _ _ □

_ _ □ □ _

_ _ □ _

□ _ _ _ _

Solve the Riddle!

It has ___ ___ ___ ___ ___ .

Name: _____ Date: _____

Write the word for each picture on the lines.
Then make a word that solves each riddle.
Use the letters in the boxes.

? ? Riddle 37   Why do bananas put on sunscreen?

_____ _____ _____ ☐

_____ ☐ _____ _____

_____ ☐ _____ _____

☐ _____ _____ _____

Solve the Riddle!

So they won't _____ _____ _____ _____ .

? ? Riddle 38   Where does spaghetti go to dance?

_____ _____ _____ _____ ☐

_____ _____ ☐ _____

_____ _____ ☐ _____

☐ _____ _____ _____

Solve the Riddle!

the _____ _____ _____ _____ – ball

Name: _____ Date: _____

Write the word for each picture on the lines.
Then make a word that solves each riddle.
Use the letters in the boxes.

?? Riddle 39 What starts with T, ends with T, and is full of T?

___ ___ ___ ___ ___ [ ]

___ [ ] ___ ___

___ ___ [ ] ___

Solve the Riddle!

a ___ ___ ___ pot

?? Riddle 40 What has an eye but can't see?

___ [ ] ___ ___

___ ___ [ ] [ ] ___

[ ] ___ ___ ___

___ ___ ___ [ ]

___ ___ [ ] ___

Solve the Riddle!

a ___ ___ ___ ___ ___ ___ ___

Name: _____ Date: _____

Write the word for each picture on the lines.
Then make a word that solves each riddle.
Use the letters in the boxes.

? ? Riddle 41 What's the best thing for hives?

☐ ___ ___ ___

___ ☐ ___ ___

___ ___ ___ ☐ ___ ___

☐ ___ ___

Solve the Riddle!

___ ___ ___ ___

? ? Riddle 42 Why did the drum take a nap?

☐ ___ ___ ___

___ ___ ___ ☐ ___

___ ___ ☐ ___

☐ ___ ___ ___

Solve the Riddle!

It was ___ ___ ___ ___ .

Name: _____ Date: _____

Write the word for each picture on the lines.
Then make a word that solves each riddle.
Use the letters in the boxes.

? ? Riddle 43 What flies without wings?

_ _ [ ] _

[ ] _ _

_ _ [ ] _

_ _ _ [ ]

Solve the Riddle!

___ ___ ___ ____

? ? Riddle 44 Why does a spider use a computer?

[ ] _ _ _

_ [ ] _

[ ] _

_ _ [ ]

Solve the Riddle!

to find a Web ___ ___ ___ ___

Name: _____ Date: _____

Write the word for each picture on the lines.
Then make a word that solves each riddle.
Use the letters in the boxes.

?? Riddle 45   Why do fireflies do well in school?

☐ ___ ___ ___

___ ☐ ___

___ ☐ ___

___ ___ ☐ ☐ ___

___ ☐ ___

Solve the Riddle!
        They are ___ ___ ___ ___ ___ ___ .

?? Riddle 46   What did the snowman say to the child?

___ ☐ ___

___ ___ ☐ ___

___ ___ ___ ☐

Solve the Riddle!
        Have an ___ ___ ___ day!

Solve-the-Riddle Phonics Practice © 2010 by Deborah Schecter. Scholastic Teaching Resources

Name: _____ Date: _____

Write the word for each picture on the lines.
Then make a word that solves each riddle.
Use the letters in the boxes.

Riddle 47   What game do bees like best?

Solve the Riddle! ____ ____ ____ ____ -and-seek

Riddle 48   What can you wear in any weather?

Solve the Riddle!   a ____ ____ ____ ____ ____

Name: _____ Date: _____

Write the word for each picture on the lines.
Then make a word that solves each riddle.
Use the letters in the boxes.

? ? Riddle 49   What has teeth but cannot bite?

☐ ___ ___ ___

___ ☐ ___ ___

☐ ___ ___ ___

___ ___ ☐ ___

Solve the Riddle!

a ___ ___ ___ ___

? ? Riddle 50   What runs for miles but never moves?

☐ ___ ___

___ ☐ ___ ___

___ ___ ☐ ___

___ ___ ___ ☐

Solve the Riddle!

a ___ ___ ___ ___

Name: _____ Date: _____

Write the word for each picture on the lines.
Then make a word that solves each riddle.
Use the letters in the boxes.

?? Riddle 51 What kind of ball will not bounce?

___ ___ [ ] ___

[ ] ___ ___ ___

___ [ ] ___ ___

___ ___ [ ] ___

Solve the Riddle!

a ___ ___ ___ ___ ball

?? Riddle 52 What gets bigger the more you take out?

___ [ ] ___ ___ ___

___ [ ] ___ ___

___ [ ] ___ ___

___ ___ ___ ___ [ ]

Solve the Riddle!

a ___ ___ ___ ___

Name: _____ Date: _____

Write the word for each picture on the lines.
Then make a word that solves each riddle.
Use the letters in the boxes.

? ? Riddle 53 What can run but does not have legs?

_____ _____ ☐ _____

_____ ☐ _____ _____

_____ _____ ☐ _____ _____

_____ _____ ☐ _____

Solve the Riddle!

your _____ _____ _____ _____

? ? Riddle 54 What kind of fish might make you rich?

☐ _____ _____ _____

_____ ☐ _____ _____

_____ _____ ☐ _____

_____ _____ ☐

Solve the Riddle!

a _____ _____ _____ _____ fish

32

Solve-the-Riddle Phonics Practice © 2010 by Deborah Schecter. Scholastic Teaching Resources

Name: _____ Date: _____

Write the word for each picture on the lines.
Then make a word that solves each riddle.
Use the letters in the boxes.

? ? Riddle 55   What is a good thing to keep in summer?

___ ☐ ___ ___ ___

___ ☐ ___

___ ☐ ___ ___

___ ___ ___ ___ ☐

Solve the Riddle!

___ ___ ___ ___ !

? ? Riddle 56   What do you call a ghost's mistake?

☐ ___ ___ ___

___ ☐ ☐ ___ ___

___ ☐ ___ ___

___ ___ ☐ ☐ ___

Solve the Riddle!

a ___ ___ ___ − ___ ___ ___

Name: _____ Date: _____

Write the word for each picture on the lines.
Then make a word that solves each riddle.
Use the letters in the boxes.

? ? Riddle 57 What do you use to clean a train's teeth?

_____ _____ _____ ☐ _____

_____ _____ ☐ _____ _____

_____ _____ ☐ _____ _____

_____ _____ _____ ☐ _____

Solve the Riddle!

_____ _____ _____ _____ _____ – paste

? ? Riddle 58 Where do cows go for fun?

☐ _____ _____ _____ _____

_____ _____ ☐ _____ _____

_____ _____ ☐ _____ _____

Solve the Riddle!

to the _____ _____ _____ – vies

34

Name: _____ Date: _____

> Write the word for each picture on the lines.
> Then make a word that solves each riddle.
> Use the letters in the boxes.

Riddle 59 What is found all over a house?

____ [ ] ____ ____

____ [ ] ____ ____

____ [ ] ____ ____

[ ] ____ ____ ____

Solve the Riddle!

a ____ ____ ____ ____

Riddle 60 Where do cars go when they get hot?

____ ____ [ ]

____ [ ] ____

____ [ ] ____

____ [ ] ____

Solve the Riddle!

to a car ____ ____ ____

Solve-the-Riddle Phonics Practice © 2010 by Deborah Schecter. Scholastic Teaching Resources

35

Name: _____ Date: _____

Write the word for each picture on the lines.
Then make a word that solves each riddle.
Use the letters in the boxes.

Riddle 61   What has two covers but no bed?

☐ ___ ___ ___

___ ☐ ___

___ ☐ ___

___ ___ ☐

Solve the Riddle!

a ___ ___ ___ ___

Riddle 62   How can you cut an ocean wave in half?

☐ ___ ___ ___

___ ☐ ___

___ ___ ☐

Solve the Riddle!

Use a sea ___ ___ ___ .

Name: _____ Date: _____

Write the word for each picture on the lines.
Then make a word that solves each riddle.
Use the letters in the boxes.

? ? Riddle 63 What has a trunk, but is not an animal?

___ [ ] ___ ___ ___

___ [ ] ___ ___

___ [ ] ___

Solve the Riddle!

a ___ ___ ___

? ? Riddle 64 Where was the bear when the lights went out?

___ ___ ___ [ ]

___ [ ] ___

___ ___ [ ] ___

___ ___ [ ] ___

Solve the Riddle!

in the ___ ___ ___ ___ !

Name: _____ Date: _____

Write the word for each picture on the lines.
Then make a word that solves each riddle.
Use the letters in the boxes.

? ? Riddle 65 What kind of fish light up the night sky?

☐ ___ ___ ___ ___

___ ___ ___ ☐

___ ☐ ___

___ ___ ☐ ___

Solve the Riddle!

___ ___ ___ ___ fish

? ? Riddle 66 What has three feet but cannot walk?

☐ ___ ___

___ ☐ ___

___ ___ ☐

☐ ___

Solve the Riddle!

a ___ ___ ___ ___

Name: _____ Date: _____

Write the word for each picture on the lines.
Then make a word that solves each riddle.
Use the letters in the boxes.

? ? Riddle 67   What sleeps with its shoes on?

□ ___ ___ ___

□ □ ___

□ ___ ___

___ ___ ___ ___ □

Solve the Riddle!

a ___ ___ ___ ___ ___

? ? Riddle 68   What is both inside a room and outside?

___ ___ ___ □

___ □ ___

___ □ ___

___ ___ □ ___

Solve the Riddle!

a ___ ___ ___ ___

Name: _____ Date: _____

Write the word for each picture on the lines.
Then make a word that solves each riddle.
Use the letters in the boxes.

?? Riddle 69 What can you hear but never see?

___ ___ ___ [ ] ___

___ [ ] ___ ___

___ [ ] ___ ___

[ ] ___ ___ ___

Solve the Riddle!

___ ___ ___ ___ e

?? Riddle 70 What has a head and a tail, but no body?

[ ] ___ ___ ___

___ [ ] ___ ___

___ ___ [ ] ___

___ ___ [ ] ___

Solve the Riddle!

a ___ ___ ___ ___

40

Name: _____ Date: _____

Write the word for each picture on the lines.
Then make a word that solves each riddle.
Use the letters in the boxes.

? Riddle 71 Why did the cat get a computer?

_____ ___ ___ ___

___ ___ ___ ___

___ ___ ___ ___ ___

___ ___ ___ ___

Solve the Riddle!

for the ___ ___ ___ ___

? Riddle 72 How do you buy a hammer?

___ ___ ___ ___

___ ___ ___ ___

___ ___ ___ ___

___ ___ ___ ___

Solve the Riddle!

by the ___ ___ ___ ___

Solve-the-Riddle Phonics Practice © 2010 by Deborah Schecter. Scholastic Teaching Resources

41

Name: _____ Date: _____

Write the word for each picture on the lines.
Then make a word that solves each riddle.
Use the letters in the boxes.

Riddle 73   Where did Humpty Dumpty go when he fell?

___ ___ ___ ___ [ ]

[ ] ___ ___

___ ___ [ ] ___

___ ___ ___ ___ [ ]

Solve the Riddle!

___ ___ ___ ___ !

Riddle 74   What gets wetter the more it dries?

[ ] ___ ___ ___ ___

___ [ ] [ ] ___

___ ___ ___ [ ] ___

___ [ ] ___ ___

Solve the Riddle!

a ___ ___ ___ ___

Name: _____ Date: _____

Write the word for each picture on the lines.
Then make a word that solves each riddle.
Use the letters in the boxes.

Riddle 75 What has five fingers but is not a hand?

Solve the Riddle!

a ___ ___ ___ ___ ___ ___

Riddle 76 What flies but never goes anywhere?

Solve the Riddle!

a ___ ___ ___ ___ ___

Name: _____ Date: _____

Write the word for each picture on the lines.
Then make a word that solves each riddle.
Use the letters in the boxes.

? ? Riddle 77 How do you make a hot dog roll?

☐ ☐ ___ ___ ___

___ ☐ ___

___ ___ ___ ☐

___ ___ ___ ___ ☐

Solve the Riddle!

Tilt your ___ ___ ___ ___ ___ .

? ? Riddle 78 What runs and runs but never gets anywhere?

☐ ☐ ___ ___

___ ☐ ___ ___

☐ ___ ___ ___

___ ___ ___ ☐

Solve the Riddle!

a ___ ___ ___ ___ ___ ___

Name: _____ Date: _____

Write the word for each picture on the lines.
Then make a word that solves each riddle.
Use the letters in the boxes.

Riddle 79 What do you call a sad berry?

☐ ___ ___ ___ ___

___ ☐ ___ ___

___ ___ ☐ ___

___ ___ ☐ ___

Solve the Riddle!
a ___ ___ ___ ___ berry

Riddle 80 What part of school does a firefly like best?

☐ ___ ___ ___

___ ☐ ___ ___

___ ___ ☐ ___ ___ ___

___ ___ ___ ☐ ___

Solve the Riddle!
___ ___ ___ ___ -and-tell

Name: _____ Date: _____

Write the word for each picture on the lines.
Then make a word that solves each riddle.
Use the letters in the boxes.

Riddle 81 Why did the cookie go to the doctor?

□ □ __ __

__ __ □ □

□ __ __ __

__ __ □ __

Solve the Riddle!

It felt __ __ __ __ – __ .

Riddle 82 What can you put in a glass but never take out?

□ □ __ __

__ __ □ __

□ __ __ __

__ __ __ □

Solve the Riddle!

a __ __ __ __ .

Name: _____ Date: _____

Write the word for each picture on the lines.
Then make a word that solves each riddle.
Use the letters in the boxes.

? ? Riddle 83 What bird can lift the most weight?

☐ ☐ ___ ___ ___

___ ___ ☐ ___ ___

___ ___ ___ ___ ☐

___ ___ ___ ___ ☐ ___

Solve the Riddle!

a ___ ___ ___ ___ ___

? ? Riddle 84 What grows down as it grows up?

☐ ☐ ___ ___

___ ___ ☐ ___

___ ___ ☐ ___ ___

Solve the Riddle!

a ___ ___ ___ ___

Name: _____ Date: _____

Write the word for each picture on the lines.
Then make a word that solves each riddle.
Use the letters in the boxes.

?? Riddle 85 What can you hold without touching?

☐ ☐ ☐ ___ ___

___ ___ ☐ ___ ___

☐ ___ ___ ___

___ ___ ___ ___ ___ ☐

Solve the Riddle!

your ___ ___ ___ ___ ___ ___

?? Riddle 86 What letter of the alphabet is a treat to eat?

☐ ☐ ☐ ___ ___

___ ___ ☐ ___

___ ___ ☐ ___

___ ___ ___ ☐

Solve the Riddle!

a ___ ___ ___ ___ ___ – ___

48   Solve-the-Riddle Phonics Practice © 2010 by Deborah Schecter. Scholastic Teaching Resources

Name: _____ Date: _____

> Write the word for each picture on the lines.
> Then make a word that solves each riddle.
> Use the letters in the boxes.

? ? Riddle 87   What is the slowest way to send a letter?

Solve the Riddle!

by U.S. ___ ___ ___ ___ ___ ___

? ? Riddle 88   What has holes but holds water?

Solve the Riddle!

a ___ ___ ___ ___ ___

Name: _____ Date: _____

> Write the word for each picture on the lines.
> Then make a word that solves each riddle.
> Use the letters in the boxes.

?? Riddle 89 What goes up and down but stays still?

Solve the Riddle!

_____

?? Riddle 90 Why do mice need oil?

Solve the Riddle!

They ____ ____ ____ ____ ____ ____ ____ !

Name: _____ Date: _____

Write the word for each picture on the lines.
Then make a word that solves each riddle.
Use the letters in the boxes.

Riddle 91 What would you get if you put butter on your bed?

☐ ☐ ☐   ___ ___

___ ___ ___ ☐ ___ ___

___ ___ ___ ☐ ___ ___

___ ___ ___ ___ ☐

Solve the Riddle!

a bed ___ ___ ___ ___ ___ ___

Riddle 92 What does a scarecrow use to drink milk?

☐ ☐ ☐   ___ ___

___ ___ ___ ☐ ___

___ ___ ___ ___ ☐

Solve the Riddle!

a ___ ___ ___ ___ ___

Name: _____ Date: _____

Write the word for each picture on the lines.
Then make a word that solves each riddle.
Use the letters in the boxes.

?? Riddle 93   What can you catch but cannot throw?

_____ ☐ _____ _____ _____

_____ ☐ _____ _____

_____ _____ ☐ _____

_____ _____ _____ ☐

Solve the Riddle!

a _____ _____ _____ _____

?? Riddle 94   What did the tub say to the water?

_____ ☐ _____ _____ _____ _____

☐ _____ _____

_____ _____ ☐ _____

_____ _____ ☐

Solve the Riddle!

I will _____ _____ _____ _____ you.

Name: _____ Date: _____

Write the word for each picture on the lines.
Then make a word that solves each riddle.
Use the letters in the boxes.

Riddle 95 Where do fish get money?

[ ] _ _ _

_ [ ] _ _

_ [ ] _

_ _ [ ]

Solve the Riddle!
at the river – ____ ____ ____ ____

Riddle 96 Why did the elephant have a bad trip?

[ ] _ _ _

[ ] _ _

_ _ [ ] _

_ _ [ ] [ ]

Solve the Riddle!
He forgot his ____ ____ ____ ____ .

Name: _____ Date: _____

Write the word for each picture on the lines.
Then make a word that solves each riddle.
Use the letters in the boxes.

?? Riddle 97 Why do cows wear bells?

___ [ ] ___ ___

___ ___ [ ] ___

___ ___ [ ]

Solve the Riddle!

Their horns don't w ___ ___ ___ .

?? Riddle 98 What goes around the world
but stays in a corner?

[ ] [ ] ___ ___

___ [ ] ___

___ ___ [ ] ___

___ ___ ___ [ ]

Solve the Riddle!

a ___ ___ ___ ___ ___

Name: _____ Date: _____

Write the word for each picture on the lines.
Then make a word that solves each riddle.
Use the letters in the boxes.

? ? Riddle 99   What has four legs but can't walk?

[ ] [ ] ___ ___ ___

___ ___ [ ] ___

___ ___ [ ] ___

___ ___ ___ [ ] ___

Solve the Riddle!

a ___ ___ ___ ___ ___

? ? Riddle 100   What do you do with a blue whale?

[ ] [ ] ___ ___ ___

___ ___ [ ] ___

___ ___ [ ] ___

___ ___ [ ] ___

Solve the Riddle!

___ ___ ___ ___ ___ her up.

Solve-the-Riddle Phonics Practice © 2010 by Deborah Schecter. Scholastic Teaching Resources

Name: _____   Date: _____

Write the word for each picture on the lines.
Then make a word that solves each riddle.
Use the letters in the boxes.

Riddle 101   What does a snake like to drink?

□ □ ___ ___

___ ___ □ ___ ___

___ ___ ___ □

___ ___ □ ___

Solve the Riddle!

a rattle ___ ___ ___ ___ ___

Riddle 102   Why did the barber win the race?

□ □ ___ ___ ___

___ ___ ___ □ ___ ___

___ ___ ___ □

___ ___ ___ □

Solve the Riddle!

He knew a ___ ___ ___ ___ cut.

Name: _____ Date: _____

Write the word for each picture on the lines.
Then make a word that solves each riddle.
Use the letters in the boxes.

?? Riddle 103 What did one pencil say to the other pencil?

Solve the Riddle!

You look ____ ____ ____ ____ ____!

?? Riddle 104 How do sailors send packages to their families?

Solve the Riddle!

They ____ ____ ____ ____ them.

Name: _____ Date: _____

Write the word for each picture on the lines.
Then make a word that solves each riddle.
Use the letters in the boxes.

? ? Riddle 105 What is on the gingerbread boy's bed?

☐ ☐ ___ ___ ___

___ ___ ☐ ___ ___

___ ___ ☐ ___ ___

___ ___ ___ ___ ☐ ___

Solve the Riddle!

a cookie ___ ___ ___ ___ ___

? ? Riddle 106 How does a turtle call its friends?

☐ ☐ ___ ___ ___

___ ___ ___ ___ ☐ ___

___ ___ ___ ☐ ___

___ ___ ___ ___ ☐

Solve the Riddle!

on a ___ ___ ___ ___ ___ – phone

Solve-the-Riddle Phonics Practice © 2010 by Deborah Schecter. Scholastic Teaching Resources

Name: _____ Date: _____

Write the word for each picture on the lines.
Then make a word that solves each riddle.
Use the letters in the boxes.

? ? Riddle 107 What goes tick-tock, bow-wow?

Solve the Riddle!

a ___ ___ ___ ___ ___ dog

? ? Riddle 108 What goes on a pumpkin when it gets a cut?

Solve the Riddle!

a pumpkin ___ ___ ___

Name: _____ Date: _____

> Write the word for each picture on the lines.
> Then make a word that solves each riddle.
> Use the letters in the boxes.

Riddle 109 Which month never walks?

_[ ] _ _ _ _
_ _ [ ] _ _ _
_ _ _ _ [ ] _
_ _ [ ] [ ] _

Solve the Riddle!
_ _ _ _ _

Riddle 110 What does a boxer like to drink?

_ [ ] _ _ _
_ _ _ [ ] _
_ _ _ [ ] _
_ _ _ [ ] [ ]

Solve the Riddle!
_ _ _ _ _

Name: _____ Date: _____

Write the word for each picture on the lines.
Then make a word that solves each riddle.
Use the letters in the boxes.

? ? Riddle 111 How are computers and waves alike?

_____ ☐ _____ _____ _____

_____ ☐ _____ _____ _____

_____ ☐ _____ _____

_____ _____ ☐ ☐

Solve the Riddle!

They can ___ ___ ___ ___ ___ .

? ? Riddle 112 What helps fireflies learn their math facts?

_____ ☐ _____ _____

_____ ☐ _____ _____

_____ _____ ☐ _____

_____ _____ ☐ ☐

Solve the Riddle!

___ ___ ___ ___ ___ cards

Solve-the-Riddle Phonics Practice © 2010 by Deborah Schecter. Scholastic Teaching Resources

Name: _____ Date: _____

Write the word for each picture on the lines.
Then make a word that solves each riddle.
Use the letters in the boxes.

?? Riddle 113 **What is the best thing to put in a pie?**

____ ____ □ ____

____ □ ____ ____

□ ____ ____

____ ____ □ □

Solve the Riddle!

your ____ ____ ____ ____ ____!

?? Riddle 114 **What did the phone say to the bell?**

____ ____ □ ____ ____ ____

____ □ ____ ____

____ □ □

Solve the Riddle!

Give me a ____ ____ ____ ____ .

Answers

Page 36
Riddle 61: a book
(brook, look, foot, hook)
Riddle 62: Use a sea saw.
(straw, draw, claw

Page 37
Riddle 63: a car
(scarf, yard, arm)
Riddle 64: in the dark!
(card, bark, farm, park)

Page 38
Riddle 65: starfish
(shark, cart, part, jar)
Riddle 66: a yard
(yarn, barn, chart, dart)

Page 39
Riddle 67: a horse
(horn, fork, snore, store)
Riddle 68: a door
(sword, corn, core, thorn)

Page 40
Riddle 69: noise
(point, boil, oil, soil)
Riddle 70: a coin
(coil, foil, soil, oink)

Page 41
Riddle 71: for the mouse
(mouth, couch, house, bounce)
Riddle 72: by the pound
(spout, flour, ground, cloud)

Page 42
Riddle 73: down!
(crowd, owl, cow, crown)
Riddle 74: a towel
(tower, gown, flower, clown)

Page 43
Riddle 75: a glove
(glass, clown, sleeve, flame)
Riddle 76: a flag
(fly, blow, clam, globe)

Page 44
Riddle 77: Tilt your plate.
(plane, clap, float, slide)
Riddle 78: a clock
(clip, glove, climb, plank)

Page 45
Riddle 79: a blueberry
(block, cloud, plug, sled)
Riddle 80: glow-and-tell
(glue, plate, flower, claw)

Page 46
Riddle 81: It felt crumb-y.
(crib, drum, brick, cry)
Riddle 82: a crack
(crab, draw, crow, trunk)

Page 47
Riddle 83: a crane
(crawl, grass, brain, bride)
Riddle 84: a tree
(train, dream, dress)

Page 48
Riddle 85: your breath
(bread, grape, tray, branch)
Riddle 86: a brown-e
(broom, crown, drink, prize)

Page 49
Riddle 87: by U.S. Snail
(snow, stamp, ski, spill)
Riddle 88: a sponge
(spoon, stove, swing, stage)

Page 50
Riddle 89: stairs
(stem, snake, swim, spears)
Riddle 90: They squeak!
(square, smell, skate, stick)

Page 51
Riddle 91: a bedspread
(spring, screen, spray, squid)
Riddle 92: a straw
(string, strap, screw)

Page 52
Riddle 93: a cold
(child, fold, bald, gold)
Riddle 94: I will hold you.
(shield, old, build, field)

Page 53
Riddle 95: at the river-bank
(bunk, frank, ink, drink)
Riddle 96: He forgot his trunk.
(think, rink, skunk, sink)

Page 54
Riddle 97: Their horns don't work.
(fork, bark, shark)
Riddle 98: a stamp
(stump, lamp, hump, jump)

Page 55
Riddle 99: a chair
(chick, chain, chip, cherry
Riddle 100: Cheer her up.
(cheese, check, cheek, church)

Page 56
Riddle 101: a rattle shake
(ship, shave, shark, shoe)
Riddle 102: He knew a shortcut.
(shell, shadow, shirt, shout)

Page 57
Riddle 103: You look sharp!
(shower, shade, shrimp, shop)
Riddle 104: They ship them.
(shin, shoe, shield, sheep)

Page 58
Riddle 105: a cookie sheet
(shawl, shed, shelf, shorts)
Riddle 106: on a shell-phone
(shark, shine, shield, shovel)

Page 59
Riddle 107: a watchdog
(witch, branch, torch, arch)
Riddle 108: a pumpkin patch
(peach, match, crutch, beach)

Page 60
Riddle 109: March
(match, catch, church, inch)
Riddle 110: punch
(peach, couch, lunch, hatch)

Page 61
Riddle 111: They can crash.
(cash, trash, wash, dish)
Riddle 112: flash cards
(fish, leash, trash, brush)

Page 62
Riddle 113: your teeth!
(bath, tenth, earth, sloth
Riddle 114: Give me a ring.
(string, king, sing)